D1017992

OUTSTANDING PEKING, SZECHWAN, CANTONESE, AND SHANTUNG DISHES.

Chinese Cooking

An Illustrated Guide

By
Ayako Namba

Grace Z. Chu
Consultant

BARRON'S/WOODBURY, N.Y.

Second printing, 1978

American edition published in 1977 by
Barron's Educational Series, Inc.
113 Crossways Park Drive
Woodbury, New York 11797

International Standard Book No. 0-8120-0823-5

Printed in Japan

Table of Contents

Introduction 4
Different Types of Chinese Cooking 5
Menu Planning 7
Table of Cooking Methods 9
Chinese Table Manners 12
When Eating 13
Beverages 14
Tea 15
Practicing Menus
        Hors d'Oeuvre 16
        Soup 20
        Vegetables 26
        Fish & Shellfish 34
        Meat & Egg 42
        Noodles & Rice 66
        Snack 72
        Dessert 78
How to Make Chinese Noodles 81
How to Prepare Noodles 82
Seasonings and Spices 83
Special Foods 86
How to Use Chopsticks 89
How to Cut the Ingredients 90
Dinner Set for Chinese Dishes 92
Utensils to Have on Hand 94
Index 97

Introduction

Although simply titled *Chinese Cooking*, this book actually includes many different types of cuisine, corresponding to the climates, customs, history, and products of the various regions of the country. I have combined the good points of the various methods of each region to suit the tastes of westerners and have adapted them for easier home cooking.

This collection of recipes is intended for those who would like to prepare Chinese food at home—whether for parties or for a family.

Do not hesitate to try any of the dishes included in this book; they need not be followed in the order given. Whichever dish you may choose to prepare, you will be able to obtain satisfactory results by following the directions. Remember, however, that in Chinese cooking, if the number of people in the dinner party increases, so does the number of dishes. Thus, if you can efficiently plan a menu from the recipes presented, you will be able to serve a meal for many guests.

An understanding of cooking is not based merely on knowledge but is acquired from experience and through the five senses. Technique itself cannot be explained beyond a certain level and further skill is acquired through practice. Try these recipes, practice your cooking, and develop an appreciation for Chinese food.

Ayako Namba

Different Types of Chinese Cooking

Many categories of Chinese cooking come from various geographical divisions of the country. They may be divided into the following four:

1. Peking and Shantung Food (North)

This is the blending of the different types of dishes brought by the court officials during the Ming and Ching Dynasties with the native dishes of the regions. This area is extremely cold in winter; thus, pork, duck, lamb, and other meats are primarily eaten. Rich foods and pot dishes are popular. The area is rich in wheat and many dishes are based on this grain, popular items being cakes, noodles, etc.

Representative dish:

北京烤鸭 (Bei-jing-kao-ya), Peking Duck

2. Szechwan Food (West)

This area is largely flat land blessed with a gentle and rather humid climate and fertile soil, which makes this region rich in agricultural products.

The food developed in the capital of the basin area is a remnant of court dishes; it is especially known for its beautifully presented hors d'oeuvre, often in the shapes of crane, turtle, etc.

The leek, garlic, red pepper, white pepper, etc., are used for seasoning vegetables.

The richness of the salt mines in the hills has led to a well-developed pickled vegetable business. This is represented by zha-cai, green.

Representative dishes:

麻婆豆腐 (Ma-po-dou-fu), Stir-fried Spiced Bean Curd and Pork

回锅肉 (Hui-guo-rou), Pork with Hot Bean Paste

3. Cantonese Food (South)

This is a subtropical region, abundant in agricultural products and seafood. Fish dishes are plentiful.

Dishes utilizing recent food products, such as ketchup or bread, are also abundant.

The main ingredients in dishes are most often marinated. A la carte dishes are more prevalent than full course dinners.

Representative dish:

芙蓉蟹 (Fu-rong-xie), Crabmeat Omelet

4. Shanghai and Hangchow (East Central)

This section of China is mild in climate and fertile in soil. It borders on both river and sea, therefore it is rich in seafoods. Very little spice is used. Soy sauce, sugar, and fresh ginger roots are usually used. The food is delicate in taste.

Representative dish:

红烧黄鱼 (Hong-shao-huang-yu), Fried and Stewed fish in soy sauce, ginger root, and scallion.

Menu Planning

There are some points you have to bear in mind when planning a menu.

1. Select dishes which will appeal to the persons involved.
2. Select dishes utilizing ingredients of the season; they are cheaper and of better quality.
3. Do not assume that expensive ingredients are best. Learn to use food economically. For example, use stock left over from other dishes or liquid used to soak dried foods in. When buying a whole chicken, plan to use gizzards, liver, legs and bones in other dishes.
4. Avoid repeating the same type of dish in a meal.
5. Select one or two dishes that will not require too much time; choose those which you have had experience in preparing.

Menu for Guests

Menu in Chinese is called 菜 单(cai-dan) or 菜 谱(cai-pu). A Chinese meal usually starts with cold hors d'oeuvre, followed by hot main dishes and finishes with soup and sweets or fruits. In the past so many dishes were prepared that one could not eat them all. The present menu, however, has been simplified, and a full course dinner consists of about 10 dishes. If eight persons are present, eight dishes may be served.

Hors d'Oeuvre : Select dishes which will not lose their flavor when cold; prepare early and set aside. There should be a wide assortment of dishes.

Main Dishes : The same type of cooking methods and

7

seasonings should not be repeated. Generally speaking, start with a lightly seasoned dish and progress to richer foods.

Dishes requiring much time and energy are most appreciated. Fish dishes are served last. At formal occasions they are served whole, deep-fried or steamed, but never cut into pieces.

Soup: Rice is served with fish, soup or pickled vegetables.

Dessert: When rice is not served, light dishes and some sweets, together with tea, are substituted.

Menu for Family

For 4 to 5 persons, soup and four dishes are enough. Of the four dishes, meat, fish, eggs and vegetable are chosen with an eye on balance: lightly seasoned dishes with richer seasoned foods. Dishes should be selected by cooking methods: cold dishes, deep-fried, sautéd, stewed and steamed foods.

For family anniversaries and festive occasions, select more elaborate dishes using chicken or fish. Add shrimps and crabs to ordinary dishes. Select those which may be reheated or eaten cold so that preparation does not take too much time.

One-Place Setting
Above: soup bowl
      wine cup
      teacup
Below: 2 small plates for food
      porcelain spoon with rest
      chopsticks or fork

Table of Cooking Methods

炒 菜 (Chao-cai), **Pan-frying or Sautéing**
1. Cut all the ingredients into the same size.
2. Heat the pan until smoking before pouring in the oil to prevent food sticking to the pan.
3. The amount of oil should be about 8 to 10% of the weight of the food.
4. Sauté minced ginger and/or garlic in the oil which is to be used for pan-frying.
5. Cook over high heat for a short time until ingredients turn color.

Various Methods

清 炒 (Qing-chao) : Pan-fry all ingredients separately or add other ingredients to the pan-fried food.

京 炒 (Jing-chao) : Pan-fry all together.

爆 炒 (Bao-chao) : Deep-fry first then pan-fry.

煎 炒 (Jian-chao) : Pan-fry in a little amount oil just until ingredients turn color.

炸 菜 (Zha-cai), **Deep-frying**
1. Heat the oil in a deep-frying pan to 355°F. Put a few drops of the batter in the oil and if you find them sink half way to the bottom of the pan then spread rapidly, the temperature is right.
2. Fresh oil should be used for foods that will not smell; you may then use again and again. For example: Use fresh oil to deep-fry shrimps and vegetables; use again for pork and finally for fish.
3. Large pieces of food must be deep-fried twice for a crispy effect.

Various Methods

清 炸 (Qing-zha) : Deep-fry without batter.

干 炸 (Gan-zha) : Deep-fry coated ingredients.

9

高　丽 (Gao-li): For a white coating, egg whites and cornstarch are used in the batter. Use fresh oil.

煨 (Wei) and 焖 (Men), **Stewed Dishes**

Fry, deep-fry or grill first for preparation and then simmer over low heat.

Various Methods

白　煨 (Bai-wei): For a white gravy, season with dry sherry, salt, sugar or vinegar.

红　煨 (Hong-wei): To the above, add soy sauce to make the gravy turn color.

烧 (Shao), **Grilling**

Generally it means cooking directly over the flame, but it also means the methods of cooking such as stewing, deep-frying, steaming, etc.

Various Methods

卤 (Lu) and 酱 (Jiang): Stew foods with gravy of salt and soy sauce until most of the liquid is reduced.

烩 (Hui): Simmer pan-fried or boiled foods in a broth and thicken with cornstarch.

锅　子 (Guo-zi): Pot dish prepared and eaten at the table.

涮 (Shuan): A variety of one pot dish where ingredients are passed through boiling water, seasoned and eaten at once.

蒸 (Zheng), **Steaming**

Fish or meat dishes are marinated, arranged on a platter and steamed over high heat. Eggs are done over low heat, cakes over strong heat.

溜 (Liu), **Dishs with thick gravy or sauce**

1. After adding cornstarch, turn down heat and cool. Do not let it get lumpy.

2. When thickened, turn off fire. If overcooked, it will be too thick; if not cooked enough, it will be watery

and floury.

3. Both gravy and food should be the same temperature.

Various Methods

糖 醋 (Jang-cu): Sweet and sour sauce.

酱 汁 (Ziang-zhi): Soy sauce or soy sauce with salt.

玻 璃 (Bo-li), 水 晶 (Shui-jiang): Clear transparent Liu without using soy sauce.

鸡 粥 (Ji-zhou): Mashed chicken is added to the sauce for flavor.

奶 溜 (Nai-liu): Milk is added.

茄 汁 (Qie-zhi): Tomato purée or ketchup is added.

烤 (Kao), **Grilling**

Cooked over direct heat. This method is comparatively rare in Chinese cooking. Grilled young pigs or duck are representative dishes.

熏 (Xun), **Smoking**

Sawdust is placed in a closed container and burned over low heat for smoked foods.

汤 菜 (Tang-cai), **Soups**

Various Kinds

清 菜 (Qing-cai): Clear soup.

川 汤 (Chuan-tang): Clear soup.

奶 汤 (Nai-tang): Non-clear soup.

荤 汤 (Hun-tang): Non-vegetable soup.

素 汤 (Su-tang): Vegetable soup.

拌 (Ban), Vinegared dishes.

冻 (Dong), Molds using gelatin substances.

Chinese Table Manners

There are no strict rules regarding meals; the main point is eating comfortably. This could be called the basis of Chinese etiquette.

At the table, the place nearest to the door is the host's. The farthest place away from the door is that of the guest(s) of honor. Guests are grouped around this table to the right and left according to importance. If you are younger than the other guests, it would be best to sit near the host. At small functions, the host himself will indicate the seating arrangement. Leave only after the guest of honor has left his seat.

How to Serve Food

Do not eat too much at the beginning of the meal. One serves himself after the guest of honor does, from the serving plate to individual small ones in the exact proportion of people seated (for example, if 8 persons are seated at the table, take as much as 1/8 of the food or less). You need not partake of food you dislike but it is considered bad manners not to eat all of the food you have taken. Use spoon or chopsticks accompanying the serving dish if any; if none, use your own porcelain spoon or chopsticks.

Do not hold your small plate but leave it on the table and place the food on it. However, in the case of foods with gravy, you may hold the small plate.

When you have taken from one platter, do not turn the turntable suddenly; watch to see if other guests are through with serving themselves from the other dishes, then gently turn.

If there is no turntable, hold platter in both hands and pass it around with care so as not to knock things over.

When Eating

You may use seasonings (soy sauce, mustard, vinegar, hot seasame oil) of your choice. When doing so, keep your left hand either on your knee or on the edge of the plate. When your dish is filled with remnants of the courses (bones or shells), your host or waiter will change it.

Liquors or Beverages
The first drink is for greeting. Even if you do not drink you must at least take a sip.

During the meal you may invite others at the table to drink.

Hors d'Oeuvre
If served on one large platter, dish out about 3 varieties. This is handled differently from other courses; as long as one is still eating hors d'oeuvre, the platter will not be taken away.

Eat leisurely but not to excess.

Non-boned or Unshelled Dishes
Remove bones and/or shells from mouth with chopsticks and lay on edge of plate.

Break up large pieces of food with chopsticks. However, whole chicken thighs or small birds should be eaten with hands. In this case, hand towels are usually passed around.

Whole Fish Dishes
The host or waiter will usually present the dish first and then divide it. Guests take some, then cut pieces themselves; pour gravy or accompanying sauce over. This is the last course.

Soup

Ladle into soup bowls until about 70% full. Eat soup ingredients with chopsticks; drink liquid with porcelain spoon.

Noodle Dishes

Do not slurp when eating noodles.

When drinking the soup, set chopsticks aside and use porcelain spoon.

When the soup is divided into small soup bowls, you may drink it straight from the bowls.

Meat or Sweet Filled Buns

Do not gulp down; break in half, then into bite-sized pieces over plate.

Beverages

Chinese liquors are made from rice, chestnuts, kaoliang, etc. The type of beverage produced is dependent on the climate and environment of the district involved. Each goes well with Chinese food.

There is much variety but Chinese spirits are mainly classified according to alcohol content; strong liquors 白 酒 (Bai-jiu) and weak 黄 酒 (Huang-jiu). Bai-jiu from Northern China is based on sorghum grain and is well known as 白 干 儿(Bai-gar-er). Liquors in this classfication include 高 粱 酒 (Gaoliang-jiu), 莲 花 酒 (Lian-hua-bai), and 茅 台 (Mao-tai).

Southern China with its warm gentle climate yields good rice harvests; the brewed liquors of this region are based on rice. 绍 兴 酒 (Shao-xing-jiu) is representative. 浙 江 省 (Zhe-jiang-sheng) liquors are the best. 老 酒 (Lao-jiu) is from this region. It is prized in the same manner as vintage wines.

When accompanying meals, it is heated like Japa-

A variety of beverage   Tea

nese sake. Those who like sweets drink it with crushed rock candy. The sugar dissolves in the heated drink. Good quality Lao-jiu is drunk straight.

Tea

There are various varieties of Chinese Tea—green tea, tea from flowers, black tea, oolong tea, medicinal tea, etc. Jasmine tea is the best-known flower tea. Other flower teas include 玫瑰花茶 (Mei-gui-hua-cha), dried roses in black tea and 菊花茶 (Ju-hua-cha), dried chrysanthemum tea. Chinese green tea resembling the highest quality Japanese green tea is also available and even more expensive.

How to Prepare Tea

Regardless of the kind of tea, the most important point is the utilization of boiling water. Prepare flower teas in the same manner as green tea: place leaves in a metal or porcelain teapot, pour in boiling water and then serve. Another method is that of using a teacup with cover and placing a pinch of tea leaves in the cup; pour in boiling water and cover. This is the correct procedure for Chinese green tea but it may be used for any tea of your choice. Leave the cover slightly ajar and drink through the opening.

Generally, flower teas are taken after meals. You may also use black tea without sugar.

Ingredients
Chicken, pork, eggs, fish vegetables, canned goods may be used. Do not have more than one of the same type of dish.

Preparation
Consider how the individual dishes will harmonize, using vinegared, stewed, deep-fried, steamed dishes for variety.

How to serve
Slice cooked foods smaller than you would for an entree; arrange for eye appeal, using tomatoes, cucumbers, lemons, parsley, canned cherries, etc., as garnishes.

1. Grilled Flavored Pork (see page 42.)
2. Vinegared Jellyfish
3. Stewed Mushrooms
4. Steamed Chicken
5. Fried Prawns
6. Stewed Eggs

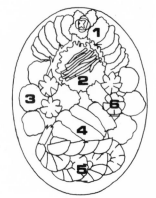

冷拼盘
(Leng-pin-pan)

Steamed Chicken

½ chicken
1 teaspoon salt
2 tablespoons dry sherry
1 scallion, cut into 2-inch pieces

1 slice ginger, crushed
2 tablespoons pan juice
2 tablespoons soy sauce
1 teaspoon sesame oil

16

冷拼盘

Method

1. Place the chicken in boiling water; when flesh turns white, rinse immediately in cold water. Remove any feathers and towel dry.
2. Set in a bowl and rub in salt and dry sherry with fingers. Place the scallion chunks and ginger on top.
3. Set the bowl in steamer over boiling water and steam over medium heat 40 minutes. When done, chop into 1-inch widths. To the pan juice, add soy sauce and sesame oil; sprinkle over chicken. Arrange skin side up.

Fried Prawns

4 large prawns	1 tablespoon dry sherry
½ teaspoon salt	2 tablespoons oil

Method

1. Remove the head, shell and black vein from the prawns.
2. Heat the oil in a pan and fry the prawns until color changes. Sprinkle on salt and dry sherry and heat for a few minutes.

Stewed Boiled Eggs

4 eggs, boiled	1 cup bouillon
4 tablespoons soy sauce	1 star anise
1 tablespoon dry sherry	4 to 5 Szechwan peppers
1 tablespoon sugar	grated

Method

1. Place the boiled eggs in water and remove shells while in the water, so they slip off easily.
2. Heat all ingredients in the stew pan and simmer for 10 minutes.

Steamed Chicken

dry sherry

salt

Fried Prawns

salt

dry sherry

Stewed Boiled Eggs

19

Oyster Soup 生蚝汤 (Sheng-hao-tang)

A tasty easy-to-prepare soup based on a stock made from shell fish. You may also use clams.

Ingredients

4 servings

½ lb. medium-sized oysters
½ teaspoon salt
2 teaspoons dry sherry
1 teaspoon ginger juice
2 tablespoons cornstarch
2 dried Chinese mushrooms or 4 fresh mushrooms
1 stalk scallion
4 cups water
1 teaspoon salt
2 teaspoons soy sauce
pinch of MSG (monosodium glutamate)
1 teaspoon sesame oil

Preparation

1. Shell oysters in a small bowl. Put in a strainer and wash them, shaking lightly in salted water.
2. Remove any broken shells which may adhere to meat. Lay the oysters on a cloth-lined colander and drain.
3. Place the oysters in a bowl and add salt, dry sherry and ginger juice; set aside for 7 to 8 minutes.
4. About 1 hour before cooking, soak dried mushrooms in water. If in a hurry, soak them in hot water for less time.
5. Remove stems; place caps right side up and slice into fine strips.
6. Cut scallion into 2- to 3-inch pieces. Slash partially

生蚝汤

1

2

3

4

5

6

ginger juice

salt

dry sherry

soy sauce

sesame oil

MSG

salt

through lengthwise and spread open. Thinly slice into fine strips. Have all ingredients ready.

Method

1. Pour water into a pot and add mushrooms. Set over high heat. When water comes to a boil, lower heat to medium.
2. Put cornstarch into a deep bowl. Lightly dredge marinated oysters with cornstarch and add to water one at a time.
3. Bring to a boil again, season with salt, pepper and MSG. Add scallion; just before done add sesame oil. Turn off heat. Pour into a large deep tureen and serve with ladle.

Notes

1. Select shelled oysters, puffy and bluish white in color. Wash just before using so as not to spoil the taste. If you are unable to obtain fresh oysters, you may use frozen or canned ones.
2. If flame is too high the soup will become cloudy and boil over. Bring to a boil over high heat, then lower to medium. Add ingredients in order and serve immediately. Do not overcook scallion and oysters or they will be limp and lose their taste.
3. To increase the amount of ingredients in the soup, you may add soft things such as bean curd. In this case, slice 4 ounces of bean curd* into chunks the same size as the oysters. Add after oysters.

* A popular food made with soy beans in China, Japan and other Oriental countries. It is high in protein and combines well with other foods.

1

2

3

Steamed Eggs 蛋蒸肉松 (Dan-zheng-rou-song)

Use a large bowl for easier cooking. This has a filling of ground pork.

Ingredients

4 servings

4 oz. ground pork
2 dried Chinese mushrooms
   or 4 fresh mushrooms
1 tablespoon oil
2 teaspoons soy sauce
¼ teaspoon salt
pinch of MSG (monosodium
   glutamate)

Egg Mixture

4 eggs
2 cups stock or water
½ teaspoon salt
pinch of MSG
½ stalk scallion
1 teaspoon seseme oil
parsley

Method

1. Soak dried mushrooms in water until soft for about an hour. Remove stems and slice thinly. Sauté in oil and crumble and add in meat. Season with salt, soy sauce and MSG.
2. Add salt and MSG to stock; beat eggs together with stock. Thinly slice scallion from smaller end and set aside.
3. Mix meat mixture and eggs together in a soup bowl.
4. Place the bowl in a steamer over boiling water and steam over medium heat until eggs turn white, then turn down heat and cook slowly until done. This usually takes about 20 minutes. Pierce the eggs with a bamboo skewer or a fork; if no liquid appears then eggs are done. Serve hot, using individual Chinese porcelain spoons.

Note

When steaming, pay attention to heat; steam gently or eggs will harden and be lumpy. About 20 minutes is sufficient cooking time for 4 servings; keep an eye on the time. Pierce with a skewer to check if done.

蛋蒸肉松

1 soy sauce
   salt
   MSG

3

2
   salt

   MSG

   4 eggs

   2 cups
   stock

   1 teaspoon
   sesame
   oil

   ½ stalk
   scallion
   parsley

4

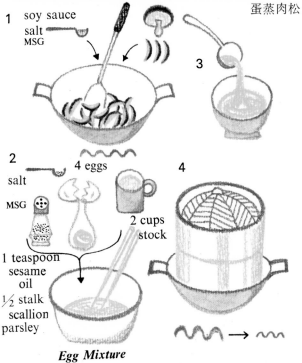

Egg Mixture

25

Chop Suey

八宝菜 (Ba-bao-cai)

A prepared dish combination of meat, fish and vegetables, depending on the ingredients used, may be served to guests or as a family meal.

Ingredients

4 servings

. 15 oz. pork

(a) {
1 teaspoon dry sherry
1½ teaspoon ginger juice
2 teaspoons cornstarch
}

4 small scallops (4 oz.)
4 oz. shelled shrimps
4 boiled quail eggs

(b) {
2 teapoons dry sherry
¼ teaspoon salt
1 teaspoon cornstarch
}

2 slices ham
2 dried Chinese mushrooms
or 4 fresh mushrooms
4 oz. bamboo shoots
3 stalks scallion
2 oz. snow peas

3 oz. vermicelli
½ teaspoon shredded ginger
4 tablespoons oil

(c) {
1 tablespoon dry sherry
1 teaspoon salt
1 tablespoon soy sauce
pinch of MSG (mono-sodium glutamate)
1 cup stock
}

2 tablespoons cornstarch dissolved in 3 table-spoons water

Preparation

1. Thinly slice pork; mix all of (a) and marinate pork in it.

2. Score scallops into crisscross and season together with shrimps and quail eggs in (b).

3. Cut each ham slice into sixths. Soak dried mushrooms in water and remove stems; slice thinly. Thinly slice bamboo shoots. Slice scallion lengthwise in ½-inch widths.

4. Clean snow peas; soak vermicelli in warm water for about 10 minutes until soft; cut into ½-inch lengths.

八宝菜

Method

1. Heat 1 tablespoon oil in a wok (or pot) over strong heat and sauté scallops, shrimps and quail eggs. Set aside.
2. Heat 3 tablespoons oil in the same pan and sauté in the following order; ginger, pork, mushrooms, bamboo shoots, scallion, vermicelli, snow peas and ham over strong heat. Return (1) and season with (c).
3. When it comes to a boil, thicken with cornstarch dissolved in water.
4. Arrange attractively on an oval platter or a flat plate; for example, set shrimps, snow peas, etc. on top. Serve immediately or vegetables will lose their flavor.

Notes

1. Be sure meat and fish are marinated since they are cooked over high heat for a short time. Vegetables requiring longer cooking time should be boiled beforehand until half done.
2. Prepare all seasonings and cornstarch before starting to cook. If overcooked, scallops will become hard and the vegetables limp.
3. This dish encompasses all kinds of food. If using many ingredients, lots of time will be involved in the preparation. For a family meal use whatever is on hand. Should the desired amount of servings be small, a variety of ingredients will be tastier.
4. You may substitute chicken, chicken gizzard and liver, boiled or deep-fried meatballs for pork. You may substitute abalone, clams, prawns for scallops and shrimps. You may use broccoli, cabbage, cauliflower, celery, cucumber, green pepper, string beans or whatever vegetable is in season.

1

2

3

4

Colorful Vinegared Dish

凉拌三丝
(Liang-ban-san-si)

This dish is attractive to the eye. An excellent example of Chinese cooking involving meticulous cutting techniques.

Ingredients

4 servings

4 thin slices ham
1 egg
pinch of salt
½ teaspoon oil
1 small cucumber
2 oz. vermicelli

Vinegar Sauce

3 tablespoons vinegar
2 tablespoons soy sauce
1 tablespoon sugar
⅓ teaspoon salt
2 teaspoons sesame oil
pinch of MSG (monosodium glutamate)

Preparation

1. Slice all ingredients thinly in long strips.
2. Prepare sauce beforehand and add just before serving. If mixed in too early, ingredients will emit water and not be colorful. This will make 4 to 6 tablespoons of sauce for 4 servings (arranged on one plate.) Add sesame oil for its distinctive fragrance.

Ham

Wash a cutting board well and towel dry. Whenever chopping or slicing, the board should be washed each time or cutting area of each ingredient kept separate so that tastes do not mix. Gently pressing ham with left hand, slice into fairly thick strips (about match stick size.) Push knife forward when cutting for a cleaner edge.

凉拌三丝

Egg Sheets

Break eggs into a bowl; add a pinch of salt. Beat well. If not thoroughly beaten, eggs will separate into white and yellow and will be lumpy. Heat a wok and grease. Test temperature by dropping a bit of egg mixture into the wok; it should sizzle. Pour in beaten eggs all at once. Shake wok to spread egg mixture over the surface of the wok. Turn over, taking care not to burn. Remove to a cutting board and slice into thin strips.

Vermicelli

Pour about 3 cups of boiling water over the vermicelli and set aside for 5 to 6 minutes. When transparent and soft, drain. Chill in cold water then cut into 2-inch lengths.

Cucumber

Holding a knife aslant, remove all rough spots from skin. Lightly squeeze with salt, rinse and cut off ends. Remove a little of the skin from greener end. Slice in 2-inch lengths diagonally. Stack a few pieces at a time and cut into thin strips.

Method

1. Heap vermicelli in the center of a plate; top with ham, cucumber and egg strips with an eye on the color scheme.
2. Just before serving pour vinegar sauce over the food.

Notes

1. Select ingredients for this dish not only for taste but also for eye appeal. For example:
   a) egg sheets, cucumber, bean sprouts
   b) ham, cucumber, jellyfish, etc. You may use as many ingredients as you desire.
2. Preparation involving sautéing and boiling are essential.
3. The ingredients cut into thin strips are easier to eat and well seasoned with the vinegar sauce.

Egg Sheets

Vermicelli

Cucumber

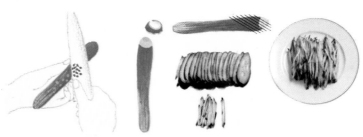

Crisp Fish with Sweet Sour Sauce　糖醋鲜鱼
(Tang-cu-xian-yu)

A fish dish with a spicy sauce and vegetables.

Ingredients

4 servings

1 bluefish (12-inch length)
2 tablespoons soy sauce
5 tablespoons cornstarch
oil for deep-frying
½ medium onion
2 oz. carrot
2 dried Chinese mushrooms or 4 fresh mushrooms
3 oz. canned bamboo shoots
1 green pepper
1 slice ginger

Sweet Sour Sauce

4 tablespoons soy sauce	
4 tablespoons vinegar	½ cup stock or water
4 tablespoons sugar	1 ½ tablespoons cornstarch
2 tablespoons ketchup	1 ½ tablespoons water

Preparation

1. Select fresh bluefish; loosen gill section. Remove entrails from "wrong side" (side which will be placed down on platter) and clean well.

2. Towel dry and make 4 or 5 slanted slits on both sides of the fish.

3. Rub entire fish with soy sauce for a better flavor and color, then dredge with cornstarch. If there is any moisture, oil will spatter.

4. Prepare onion, carrot, soaked and cleaned Chinese mushrooms, bamboo shoots and green pepper as shown in the photo. Finely mince ginger.

5. Mix together all ingredients for sauce except cornstarch, which should be dissolved in water and set aside.

糖醋鲜鱼

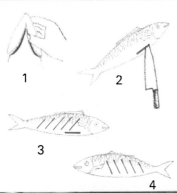

1

2

green pepper

dried Chinese mushrooms

onion

bamboo shoots

carrot

3

4

Sweet Sour Sauce

Method

1. Heat oil to 370°F in a wok or a deep frying-pan. Deep-fry fish over heat until bubbles subside (temperature of oil will be reduced to 355°F.) Lower heat to medium and cook thoroughly. Drain well. If oil overheats, remove the pan from flame until temperature drops. Should fish rise to surface of the oil, spoon oil with a ladle over until done for even cooking.

2. Heat oil in a pan and rapidly sauté ginger, carrot, mushrooms, bamboo shoots and green pepper in this order. Add seasonings and thicken with corn-starch mixture when vegetables are tender.

3. Reheat oil and return fish to deep-fry; cook until crisp.

4. Arrange fish on a platter right side up and spread sauce over.

Note

Prepare sauce and fish at about the same time. Pour over the sauce which is still bubbling.

Oil for Deep-frying

A lot of oil is used in Chinese deep-frying; strain it after using and use it again in pan-frying. Oil used to deep-fry meat is especially good in sautéing vegetables.

While oil is still warm, strain. Place a strip of cotton or paper towel over strainer to catch remnants of the coating, and gently pour oil into strainer.

Pour cleaned oil into a porcelain jar or into a bottle. Cover and set in a cool place. Lard is used mainly in fried rice and only the amount needed is made at a time. It is rarely used for deep-frying. When cooled, it turns white.

After using, clean and keep lard in a porcelain jar with cover apart from other types of grease. In hot weather, store it in the refrigerator. Old lard turns rancid so use it up as soon as possible.

1

Cook until crisp.

2

Heat oil to 370°F and
then lower to 355°F.

3

Rapidly sauté over
high heat.

4

Spread sauce over
while fish is very hot.

37

Shrimps with Green Peas 　　　青豆虾仁
(Qing-dou-xia-ren)

An eye appealing dish with an Oriental flavor.

Ingredients

4 servings

11 oz. shrimp
(a) { 1 teaspoon ginger juice
2 teaspoons dry sherry
⅓ teaspoon salt
1½ tablespoons cornstarch
1 lb. fresh green peas or 8 oz. canned green peas
1 tablespoon salt
½ stalk scallion
1 tablespoon sherry
1 teaspoon sugar
1 teaspoon salt
3 tablespoons oil

Preparation
1. When fresh green peas are used, shell the peas, wash and drain. Add salt and mix well; set aside 5 or 6 minutes. Add to boiling water and cook uncovered until tender (about 5 minutes.) Soak in ice water. If using canned peas, drain and soak in hot water to remove tinny taste. Drain. If using frozen peas, prepare according to directions on package.
2. Shell shrimps and clean. Mix in (a). Cut scallion in half lengthwise and slice in ½-inch pieces.

青豆虾仁

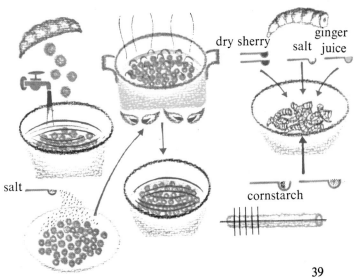

dry sherry

ginger
salt juice

salt

cornstarch

Method

1. Heat oil in a pan and rapidly sauté marinated shrimps over high heat.
2. When shrimps turn color, add scallion and green peas. Season with sherry, sugar and salt. When done, remove from heat.

Variations

1. Substitute soy beans for green peas for *Shrimps with Soy Beans.*
2. Substitute chicken for shrimps for *Chicken with Green Peas.*

Note

Do not overseason or cook shrimps too long.

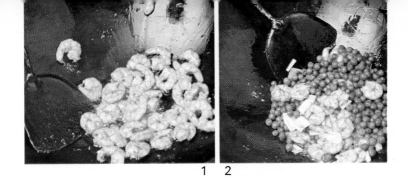

毛豆虾仁
(Mao-dou-xia-ren)

青豆鸡丁
(Qing-dou-ji-ding)

41

Grilled Flavored Pork

叉烧肉
(Cha-shao-rou)

May be used in many other dishes; three methods are given here. Test to see which suits you best.

Ingredients

4 servings

1 lb. pork
1 stalk scallion
1 slice ginger
(a) { 5 tablespoons soy sauce
2 tablespoons dry sherry
3 tablespoons sugar
dash of MSG (monosodium glutamate)
1 tablespoon sugar
1 tablespoon oil
parsley

Preparation

1. Cut meat in half along the grain; cut scallion into 2-inch pieces and crush. Crush ginger.
2. Marinate meat in a bowl with ginger, scallion and (a) for 5 hours, turning frequently.

叉烧肉

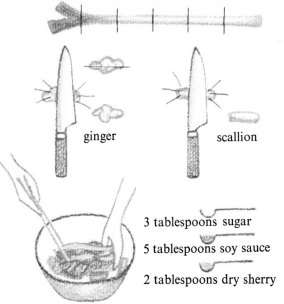

ginger

scallion

3 tablespoons sugar

5 tablespoons soy sauce

2 tablespoons dry sherry

Method

Grill over Gas

1. Heat wire grill over high heat and place drained meat on top. Too strong a flame will burn the surface before meat is fully cooked so turn heat to low.

2. When nicely browned, turn over. Using aluminum foil or metal bowl, cover and steam meat.

3. Heat (a) and add 1 tablespoon sugar for sauce. When meat is almost done, brush meat with sauce 2 to 3 times. Pierce meat with a skewer; if no red liquid appears, then meat is done (about 20 minutes).

In Chinese Wok

1. Heat oil in a wok and fry meat, turning constantly, over medium heat until evenly browned.

2. Add ½ cup water to (a) and pour into the wok. Cover (a heavy porcelain cover is preferable) and simmer for 30 minutes.

Oven Grilling

1. Heat oven to 350°F; lay meat and grill over foil covered roasting pan and place on middle shelf of the medium hot oven.

2. Brush sauce on meat as shown in the pictures and roast for about 30 minutes.

Notes

1. If meat is overcooked it will become hard. Pierce meat with a skewer to test for doneness and if no juice seeps out, meat is done. If in doubt, slice through the thickest portion; if meat is white, remove from heat. Cool until it can be held in the hand. Slice.

2. Fresh ham or pork butt, where some fat is present, is best. Buy meat whole; have your butcher cut off a section along the grain for you. After cooking, slice across the grain to yield a tenderer dish.

Grill over Gas   In Chinese Wok

Sweet Sour Pork   咕咾肉 (Gu-lao-rou)

A representative dish of rich crisp cooked pork.
Prepare in advance and be sure to cook well.

Ingredients

4 servings

1 pound pork (butt or loin)
1 tablespoon dry sherry / 1 tablespoon soy sauce
2 tablespoons cornstarch
½ onion
3 dried Chinese mushrooms or 6 fresh mushrooms
½ carrot
2 green peppers
2 thin slices pineapple
2 tablespoons oil

Sauce

⎧ 3 tablespoons vinegar   ⅓ tablespoon cornstarch
⎪ 3 tablespoons soy sauce   dissolved in 2 table-
⎨ 5 tablespoons sugar   spoons water
⎩ ½ teaspoon salt   oil for deep-frying

Preparation

1. Slice meat into 1-inch squares. Marinate in mixture of dry sherry and soy sauce for 7 to 8 minutes, then add cornstarch. Mix well.

2. Slice onions lengthwise, then into thirds, then in half. Soak mushrooms and wash. Cut into four or six pieces.

3. Slice carrot first lengthwise then into triangles. Boil until tender and set aside. Quarter green peppers, then remove seeds and stems. Slice again into three or four pieces. Slice pineapple into fourths.

4. Prepare sauce in a bowl. Set cornstarch and all vegetables together near at hand.

5. Heat oil to 355°F and deep-fry meat, adding one at a time until thoroughly cooked.

咕咾肉

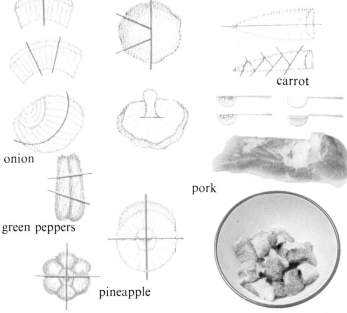

carrot

onion

pork

green peppers

pineapple

47

Method

1. Heat oil in a wok and cook over high heat in this order; mushrooms, onions, carrots, green peppers.
2. When green peppers are a beautiful green, add sauce mixture.
3. When done, add deep-fried meat, then the cornstarch dissolved in water. Cook until thicken.
4. Lastly add pineapples and stir quickly. Do not overcook.

Notes

1. You need not use fresh oil. Be sure, however, to have enough oil on hand. If the temperature of oil is too high, meat will burn before it is fully cooked. Be sure to have oil at 355°F and cook to brown evenly. Using chopsticks, keep turning meat to expose to the air for a crisper texture. Test for doneness by inserting a fork into the largest piece. If overdone, meat tends to be spongy and lose its flavor.
2. If deep-fried meat is set aside and cooled in the process, it will lose crispness as moisture comes out from inside, so try to prepare it all at once. If deep-fried beforehand, deep-fry once more.
3. If the meat is cooked longer after adding sauce, coating on meat will come apart and be sticky. Cook just enough so that each piece is coated with sauce.

Set all ingredients
near at hand.

Oriental Crisp Chicken 炸鸡块 (Zha-ji-kuai)

Marinated chicken is deep-fried for a simple, tasty dish. It may be coated with cornstarch before cooking.

Ingredients

4 servings

1 young chicken with bone
½ stalk scallion
1 slice ginger
3 tablespoons soy sauce
1½ tablespoons dry sherry
oil for deep-frying
2 medium tomatoes
parsley
½ lemon
Szechwan pepper salt

Preparation

1. Chop chicken into 1- to 2-inch pieces.
2. Cut scallion into 1-inch chunks and crush with the flat side of a knife as illustrated.
3. Marinate chicken, scallion, ginger, soy sauce and dry sherry in a bowl and set aside 30 to 40 minutes. Turn several times.

炸鸡块

1

2

3

51

Method

1. Pour oil into a wok or deep-frying pan until a little more than half full. Heat over high flame. Turn chicken all at once into a colander and drain; put chicken pieces into wok one at a time. When all have been added, lower heat to medium; stir constantly with cooking chopsticks so that chicken may be cooked faster and lightly colored. If oil is too hot, chicken will acquire a burned coating. If oil is not hot enough, on the other hand, juices will escape with long cooking and chicken will lose taste.

2. As chicken is cooked, bubbles will gradually disappear. Meat will be firm and pull apart from bones. Finally turn up heat. When oil is hot remove chicken. This is important to the cooking process. As oil is heating during this stage, quickly remove chicken with a wire strainer.

Notes

1. When prepared as a meal for guests, deep-fry chicken until lightly brown at first. Just before serving, cook again for a short time to serve while hot.

2. *Chicken*
Since the meat is tender and easy to digest, it is often used in Chinese dishes. A creamy pink bird slightly resilient to the touch is preferred. For a richer and sweeter flavor be sure to marinate before cooking.

3. *Frying Oil*
You may use regular vegetable oil. Be sure there is enough to cook all of the chicken; for about 1 pound of chicken, you will need 5 cups of oil at least.

4. *Seasoned Salt*
Mix salt and Szechwan pepper in equal amounts.

1

2

1. Pour oil in a wok until a little more than half full. Heat over high flame. When all chicken pieces have been added, lower heat to medium.
2. When chicken is cooked, bubbles will disappear.

Crisp Meatballs 炸肉丸子 (Zha-rou-wan-zi)

A basic meatball recipe; may be used in various ways—as a dish in itself with sauce, in soups, etc.

Ingredients

4 servings (*25 meatballs*)

1 lb. ground pork
1 teaspoon chopped ginger
1 tablespoon dry sherry
⅔ teaspoon salt
1 egg
dash of MSG (monosodium glutamate)
2 tablespoons cornstarch
oil for deep-frying
5 leaves lettuce
Szechwan pepper salt
mustard

Preparation

1. Ground meat twice. If twice-ground meat is not available, place on a cutting board and chop repeatedly. Fatty meat is rather tastier; ideally meat should consist of ⅘ pork loin and ⅕ rib portion. If meat contains too much fat, meatballs will shrink and lose their shape.
2. Place meat in a bowl and add seasonings as illustrated. Be sure to mix in cornstarch evenly.

Seasoned Meat
Fundamentally, add spicy ingredients before all others. Add ginger and dry sherry, then egg. Season with salt and MSG and mix until paste-like. Then quickly mix in cornstarch.

炸肉丸子

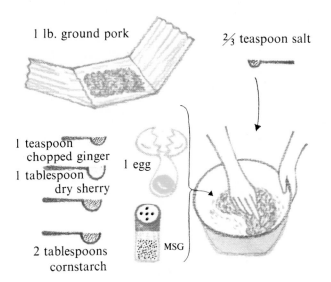

1 lb. ground pork

⅔ teaspoon salt

1 teaspoon
chopped ginger

1 tablespoon
dry sherry

1 egg

MSG

2 tablespoons
cornstarch

How to Shape Meatballs

1. Moisten left hand with water and lightly squeeze meat.
2. Squeeze the meat out of the hand to make a ball one by one as illustrated.
3. Remove the meat with a spoon that has been greased. Meatballs should be rounded, 1 inch in diameter. Drop in the middle of a pan filled with hot oil and deep-fry.

Method

1. Pour oil into a Chinese wok or deep-frying pan until about ¾ full and heat to 355°F over medium heat. Quickly add meatballs one by one.
2. When a little brown, use chopsticks to move meat from right to left until brown on all sides.
3. When meatballs are cooked and oil is no longer bubbling, remove meatballs with a strainer.

Notes

Do not add too many vegetables. When deep-frying, vegetables tend to cook faster than the meat and may burn. Be sure that ginger is finely minced or grated before adding to the meat. Mix well then add cornstarch. If oil is overheated, surface of meatballs will be burned and will be hard before interior is fully cooked. Turn meatballs with chopsticks while cooking slowly over medium heat.

Variations

a. One-Pot Dish

Cook meatballs in stock, together with quail eggs and assorted vegetables, at the table.

b. Sweet Sour Meatballs

With sour sauce, meatballs may substitute for pork.

c. Meatball Soup

A filling soup.

How to Shape Meatballs   ## *To Deep-fry*

1

2

3

1

2

3

57

Chinese Pot   什锦火锅子 (Shi-jin-huo-guo-zi)

Called "Huo-guo-zi." A special type of dish prepared at the table, consisting of many ingredients. You may use an earthenware pan.

Ingredients

4 servings

Meat Dumplings
7 oz. ground pork
½ teaspoon chopped ginger
½ tablespoon dry sherry
1 egg
⅓ tablespoon salt
2 tablespoons cornstarch
3½ oz. oysters
5 oz. shrimp
12 fresh quail eggs (or canned)
7 leaves cabbage
1 cup spinach
6 dried Chinese mushrooms or 12 fresh mushrooms

½ cup of bamboo shoots
20 gingko-nuts
1 oz. vermicelli

Soup
6 cups stock in which oysters and shrimps are cooked
2 bouillon cubes
1 teaspoon salt
2 tablespoons dry sherry
mustard to taste
vinegar to taste
soy sauce to taste

Preparation

1. Place oysters in a colander and wash in slightly salted water to get rid of their sediment. Parboil and drain, setting liquid aside.

2. Remove the head, shell and black vein from shrimps. Parboil and reserve liquid.

3. Boil cabbage until tender; parboil spinach, wash and squeeze out liquid. Lay spinach pieces alongside each other, stalk of one against leafy section of the other, and cut in half. Cut three cabbage leaves (to line bottom of pan) lengthwise into 2-inch widths. Group remaining leaves in sets of

什锦火锅子

two, laying stalk portion of one against leafy portion of the other and place on a napkin. Arrange spinach in middle of each and roll up.

4. Cut cabbage rolls into 1-inch widths.

5. See pages p. 61 through p. 64 for directions on meatballs.

6. Boil quail eggs for 5 minutes and soak in water; shell in water. (Omit this step if canned eggs are used)

7. Wash fresh mushrooms and remove stems. If using dried mushrooms, soak in water, remove stems and cut in half. Reserve liquid for soup.

8. Thinly slice lengthwise tender portion of bamboo shoots. Slice harder section thinly horizontally.

9. Shell gingko-nuts, using the blunt edge of a chopping knife or a hammer. Bring to a boil 1 cup water and $\frac{1}{2}$ teaspoon salt. Add gingko-nuts and boil, stirring constantly. When they have turned a translucent green, drain and remove skin.

10. Soak vermicelli in warm water for 10 minutes until soft. Drain and cut in 3-inch lengths.

11. Combine liquid from seafood, mushroom liquid, if any, bouillon cubes and seasonings. Heat.

Method

1. Line bottom of earthenware pan with cabbage leaves and arrange other ingredients on top, keeping an eye out for color. Remainder of ingredients should be kept close by.

2. Pour in soup; when cooked, serve direct from the pan. Remaining soup should be set aside on the table; when level of soup has gone down, add more.

3. As contents are used up, add remaining ingredients a little at a time.

4. Add soy sauce or salt, if needed. You may serve with mustard, vinegar, pepper, etc.

Egg Foo Yung
(Crabmeat Scrambled with Eggs)

芙蓉蟹 (Fu-rong-xie)

A Cantonese egg dish popular throughout China. You may prepare in individual servings if you wish.

Ingredients

4 servings

4 oz. canned crabmeat
1 stalk scallion
2 dried Chinese mushrooms or 4 fresh mushrooms
6 eggs
1 tablespoon green peas
2 teaspoons dry sherry
1 teaspoon sugar
⅓ teaspoon salt
dash of MSG (monosodium glutamate)
4 tablespoons oil

Foo Young Sauce
½ cup stock
2 teaspoons sugar
⅙ teaspoon salt
dash of MSG
1 teaspoon cornstarch
2 teaspoons water
1 tablespoon green peas

Preparation

1. Pick through crabmeat and flake.
2. Slice scallion diagonally in ⅟₁₀-inch thicknesses.
3. Soak mushrooms in water, remove stems and slice thinly.
4. Heat 1½ tablespoons oil in a wok and sauté mushrooms and scallion. Add crabmeat. Stir quickly

62

芙蓉蟹

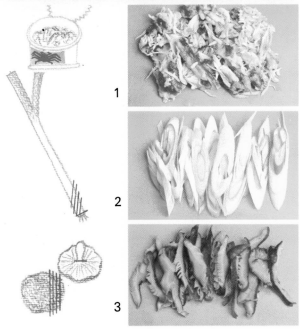

1

2

3

63

and set aside.

5. Lightly beat eggs in a bowl; add dry sherry, sugar, salt, MSG, green peas and sautéd mushroom mixture. Do not overbeat or resulting dish will not be fluffy. Beat carefully so that whites and yolks do not separate.

6. Prepare sauce; mix seasonings with stock and thicken with cornstarch dissolved in water. Add green peas.

Method

1. Heat pan over high heat; add 2½ tablespoons oil, shaking pan to distribute oil evenly. When hot, pour in egg mixture all at once. Use Chinese scoop to spread mixture and gently mix in large hand motions.

2. When half done, assemble the mixture in center of the pan. If eggs are overcooked, it will be hard to assemble. When one side is slightly brown, use scoop to turn over and cook over low heat. Do not overcook eggs or they will not be fluffy. A more skillful method involves shaking pan with one large motion to turn over omelet.

3. Remove eggs to serving dish; cut into fourths and pour sauce over eggs. A shallow dish will enhance the appearance of this dish.

Note

For Individual Servings

Divide ingredients into individual bowls and prepare as above one by one. You may also prepare whole as above. When half done, divide into individual portions with Chinese scoop, giving attention to the circular shapes.

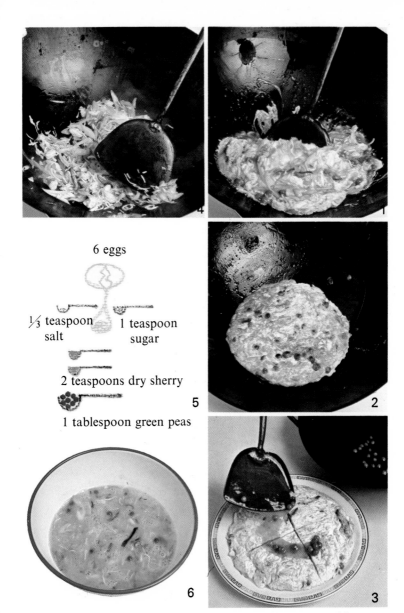

6 eggs

1/3 teaspoon salt

1 teaspoon sugar

2 teaspoons dry sherry

1 tablespoon green peas

Chow Mein
(Fried Noodles)

炒面 (Chao-mian)

This soft fried noodle dish gets its flavor from the assorted vegetables and meat. Take care not to overcook vegetables.

Ingredients

4 servings

1 lb. fresh Chinese egg noodles or narrow egg noodles
5 oz. pork, in shreds
4 oz. shelled shrimp
4 oz. carrot, in shreds
2 leaves cabbage, in shreds
1 medium onion, in shreds
5 oz. bean sprouts
2 tablespoons fungus
2 oz. snow peas
6 tablespoons oil
1 teaspoon salt
dash of pepper
3 tablespoons soy sauce
1 tablespoon sesame oil
dash of MSG (monosodium glutamate)

Method

1. Sauté pork in hot oil; add carrots. When tender add shrimps and onion and cook rapidly over high heat.
2. Mix in fungus. Add noodles, stirring well. Mix in cabbage, bean sprouts, snow peas and cook over high heat.
3. Add salt and pepper; pour soy sauce around edge of pan. Mix thoroughly with chopsticks or a Chinese scoop. Season with sesame oil and MSG.

How to Make Chinese Noodles and *How to Prepare Chinese Noodles* are described on pages 81 and 82.

炒面

1

2

3

Fried Rice with Egg   蛋炒饭 (Dan-chao-fan)

An easy-to-prepare dish. The more ingredients there are, the better the flavor.

Ingredients

4 servings

2½ cups raw rice
3 cups water
3 eggs
pinch of salt
dash of MSG (monosodium glutamate)
1 stalk scallion
2 tablespoons green peas
2 slices ham (⅓-inch thick)
5½ tablespoons lard or vegetable oil
1 teaspoon salt
1 tablespoon pepper
pinch of pepper

Preparation

1. Rinse the rice 2 or 3 times and add it to water in a casserole. Place the casserole over high heat. When the water begins to boil, reduce the heat to low. Cover the casserole tightly and simmer for about 15 minutes until all the liquid is absorbed, or cover and place in the oven and cook for 10 to 15 minutes until the rice is fluffy and dry.
2. Break eggs into a bowl and beat. Lightly season with salt and MSG.
3. Wash scallion and cut in half; thinly slice into ⅛-inch pieces from white section.
4. Dice ham into ⅛-inch pieces.
5. Drain peas, if canned, and soak in boiling water to remove tinny smell and drain immediately. In the case of frozen peas, follow directions on package.
6. Stir the rice with a fork and set aside.
7. Have seasonings and all ingredients close at hand.

蛋炒饭

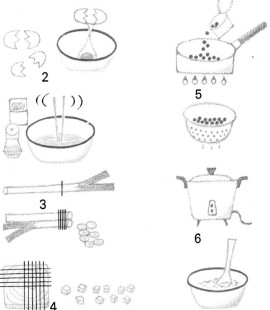

2

5

3

4

6

Method

1. Heat 1½ tablespoons lard in a Chinese wok. Pour in eggs all at once, stirring vigorously with a ladle. Cook until fluffy over high heat and remove to a plate.
2. Heat 4 tablespoons lard in the same pan. Add rice and cook over medium heat. When heated, season with salt and pepper. Add scallion, ham and green peas.
3. Push rice to one side and add soy sauce. Mix in rapidly with rice.
4. Roughly mix in eggs and remove from heat.

Notes

1. No matter how good the ingredients are, very soft rice will destroy the flavor. When using cold rice, prepare ingredients beforehand and set aside; then fry cold rice first, and return the other ingredients to pan, mixing in well.
2. If the amount of rice seems to be too much for the pan to accommodate, divide into 2 to 3 portions and cook accordingly. It is easiest to prepare for 2 servings at a time. Four servings are the maximum.

How to Render Lard

Dice leaf lard into ½-inch thin pieces. Soak in water and drain. Place in a wok stirring over high heat until fat melts. Turn heat down to medium and continue cooking until pieces of fat, which will not melt, turn brown and rise to the surface. Remove with a wire strainer. Before melted fat has cooled and hardened, pour into a container (porcelain enamel container with cover is best.) Let cool before placing in refrigerator. It is better to do this from time to time than to use a batch that has been stored for a long time.

Shao Mai
(Steamed Meat Dumplings)

烧卖 (Shao-mai)

Easy to prepare, delicious dish.

Ingredients

1 cup boiling water
4 servings

Filling

11 oz. ground pork
⅓ teaspoon salt
1 tablespoon sugar
1 tablespoon dry sherry
1 tablespoon sesame oil
dash of MSG (monosodium
glutamate)

3½ oz. onion
3 tablespoons cornstarch
1 oz. dried shrimp
2 tablespoons green peas
mustard

Preparation

1. When ground meat is used, keep in mind that meat with too much fat will shrink while cooking.
2. Slice onion in half lengthwise. Place cut side down with root end at left. Cut lengthwise, then horizontally and mince. Sprinkle with cornstarch.
3. Rinse dried shrimps in water, set aside for 10 minutes, then finely mince.
4. Mix in seasionings with meat, add onion and shrimps. Mix well. Add green peas.

Method

1. Holding wrapper (see pages 74–75) in left hand, place 1 tablespoon filling in each.
2. Lightly squeeze to shape.
3. Level off top, allowing green peas to peep through.
4. Shape as illustrated on the back cover.
5. Pour water into a wok and heat. Lightly grease a bamboo steamer rack and arrange shao mai.
   Place the steamer over boiling water in the wok and steam for 10 to 13 minutes over medium heat.
   Prepare ground mustard and set aside for serving.

烧卖

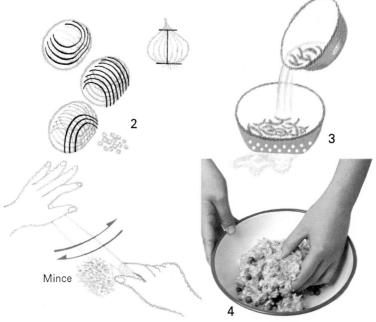

2

3

Mince

4

73

Notes

1. If heat is too high, wrapper will come apart and the shao mai will lose their shape. If water in wok evaporates too quickly, the bottom of the steamer will burn, so check often and add boiling water as needed. When there are more shao mai than the steamer will accommodate, add another layer of steamer on top.

Shao Mai Wrappers

Ingredients

30 to 40 wrappers

1 cup flour
$\frac{1}{3}$ teaspoon salt
4 tablespoons water
little cornstarch wrapped in gauze

Method

1. Mix sifted flour and salt in a bowl. Add a little boiling water and mix rapidly with a rubber spatula.
2. Knead well with hands until smooth and soft.
3. Wrap in a wet cloth and set aside for 20 minutes. When fairly sticky, it will be easier to handle.
4 – 8. Sprinkle cornstarch over pastry board, knead dough once more and roll out. Sprinkle with cornstarch and roll up away from you onto the rolling pin. Then roll out as illustrated; repeat with the under side. Open up and sprinkle with cornstarch, roll up in rolling pin, remove pin and roll out again and again. Repeat this method until dough is $\frac{1}{10}$-inch thick.
9–10. Fold until 3 inches wide, as shown in the photo, and cut into 3-inch widths.
11–12. Layer all on top of each other and cut again into 3-inch widths to square wrappers.

Steaming shao mai
in a Bamboo
steamer

How to Make Shao Mai Wrappers

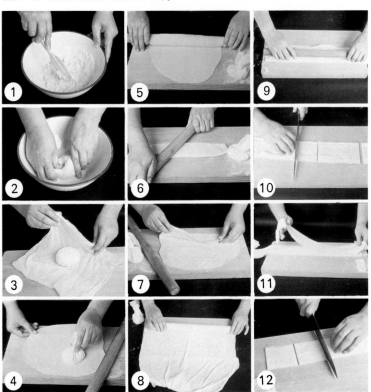

Crisp Shrimp Cakes 虾仁吐司 (Xia-ren-tu-si)

Bread combined with shrimp paste in a crisp dish.

Ingredients

4 servings

4 oz. shelled shrimp
pinch of salt
3 oz. white fish
2 oz. leaf lard
1 scallion, white portion
½ teaspoon ginger juice
2 teaspoons dry sherry
⅔ teaspoons salt
1 teaspoon sugar
dash of MSG (monosodium
glutamate)
3 tablespoons cornstarch
3 slices bread (⅔-inch
thick each)
2 teaspoons black sesame
seeds
1 slice ham
parsley
oil for deep-frying
black peppercorn salt

Preparation

1. Bone fish, set skin side down and scrape off meat. Chop.
2. Finely mince leaf lard, then scallion.
3. Wash shelled shrimps in salt water and drain. Mash with the blunt edge of chopping knife.
4. Combine shrimps, fish and lard in a bowl. Add scallion, ginger juice, dry sherry, salt, sugar, MSG and cornstarch. Mix well until sticky paste is formed.

Method

1. Remove crust from bread slices; cut one slice into four pieces, cut out second slice into 4 circles and leave remaining one whole. Spread shrimp paste on each piece. Garnish with black sesame, ham and minced parsley as illustrated. Gently press. Heat oil to 355°F over medium heat; add bread slices filling side down.
2. When slightly brown, turn over and cook until golden. Cut the whole slice of bread into several strips and arrange on a platter. Serve with black peppercorn salt.

虾仁吐司

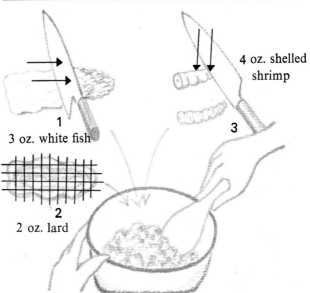

1
3 oz. white fish

2
2 oz. lard

4 oz. shelled
shrimp

3

Almond Flavored Gelatin 杏仁豆腐
(Xing-ren-dou-fu)

Instead of the Chinese flavoring, XING REN, almond extract and milk are used in this sweet smooth dessert, which is served cold.

Ingredients

4 servings

2 envelopes gelatin or 1 agar-agar
1 cup water
2 cups milk
½ cup sugar
1 teaspoon almond extract

Syrup
1 cup sugar
2 cups water

Fruits
1 canned mixed fruits
8 cherries, canned

Preparation
1. Dissolve gelatin or soak agar-agar in water 2 hours.
2. Dissolve sugar in water over low heat to obtain syrup; let cool.
3. Dice fruits; warm milk and set aside.

Method:
1. Place gelatin or agar-agar in a pot and add water and heat.
2. When dissolved, add sugar and strain.
3. Return strained gelatin or agar-agar to pot and stir in milk and almond extract.
4. Moisten mold with water and pour in contents. Refrigerate over one hour, then cut into 1-inch diamond-shaped pieces.
5. Serve with syrup and prepared fruits.

杏仁豆腐

鸡蛋糕

高丽香蕉

Steamed Cakes

鸡蛋糕
(Ji-dan-gao)

Ingredients

3 eggs
1 cup sugar
1 cup flour or rice flour
3 tablespoons raisins
1 oz. leaf lard
1 tablespoon flour
little flour for sprinkling

little oil for greasing
  custard cups
5 thin slices potato,
  shredded
dash of red food coloring
dash of blue food coloring

Method

1. Chop raisins and leaf lard. Mix in 1 tablespoon flour.
2. Soak potatoes in water and dye with blue and red food coloring.
3. Grease custard cups and sprinkle with flour.
4. Whip egg whites in a bowl until stiff. Add yolks mixed with sugar. Lightly mix in flour then raisin mixture. Fill prepared custard cups ⅘ full. Lay colored potato strips atop and steam for 10 minutes.

Frosty Bananas

高丽香蕉
(Gao-li-xiang-jiao)

Ingredients

2 bananas
1 tablespoon sugar
1 egg white
2 tablespoons water

3 tablespoons cornstarch
2 tablespoons flour
oil for deep-frying
3 tablespoons powdered sugar

Method

1. Peel bananas and cut into 2-inch lengths, then in half lengthwise and sprinkle with sugar.
2. Beat egg whites until stiff in a dry bowl and set aside. Mix sifted cornstarch and flour with water and lightly mix into egg whites.
3. For a fluffy white coating, heat fresh oil to 355°F. Dip each slice in coating and drop into hot oil.
4. Cook over low heat and turn over. When puffy, remove; sprinkle with powdered sugar while hot.

How to Make Chinese Noodles

Ingredients

4 servings

1 lb. flour ($\frac{1}{2}$ lb. high-gluten flour plus $\frac{1}{2}$ lb.
  regular flour)
1 teaspoon salt
2 teaspoons baking soda
1 egg, beaten (optional)
$\frac{2}{3}$ cup warm water
some flour for sprinkling over board

Method
1. Mix baking soda and salt with flour and then sift. Place in a large mixing bowl. Mix together egg and water, add to flour and knead well.
2. If there is enough time, wrap in cloth and set aside 20 to 30 minutes. Knead again for a softer dough.
3. Sprinkle some flour on a dough board and roll out dough very thin. Dough tends to be soft and will stick to the hand. Sprinkle with flour little by little from time to time. When $\frac{1}{10}$ inch thick, fold and cut from the edge; separate into individual strips.
4. Put noodles in a large pot of boiling water. Just before it returns to a boil, add some water and boil noodles until desired consistency. For cold noodle dishes, soak in water after cooking. Drain before use. For use in soups, add noodles directly to soup which has been poured out beforehand into individual bowls.

How to Prepare Noodles

Fresh Noodles

Bring about 15 cups of water to a boil in a large pot. Add 3 to 4 bundles of noodles, loosening them before. Bring to a boil again and add 1 cup of water. Boil, using chopsticks or a fork to separate noodles. When noodles have floated to the top, drain.

Dried Noodles

Prepare in the same way as above but add 2 cups of water instead of 1 cup. Simmer over low heat until cooked thoroughly.

Steamed Noodles

These are often used in fried noodle dishes. For noodles with soup, soak in hot water 2 to 3 minutes, separate with chopsticks; when soft, drain.

Notes

1. When a shallow pot is used, it should be wide. The most ideal one is a large pot that allows noodles to rise to the surface of the water in one layer.
2. If pot is too small, divide the noodles in half.

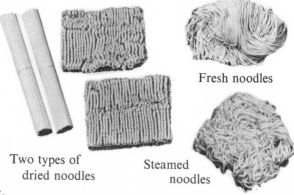

Two types of dried noodles

Fresh noodles

Steamed noodles

Seasonings and Spices

Salt, sugar, soy sauce, soybean paste, vinegar, dry sherry, monosodium glutamate and vegetable oil are commonly used in Chinese home cooking. The following seasonings and spices are typical to Chinese cooking.

Fermented Bean Curd
腐 乳 (Fu-ru)

Red and white varieties are available. This goes well with hot rice or as a seasoning with pot dishes. The red variety is also used in sautéd or stewed dishes. It is available in cans, bottles or small jars.

Fermented Black Beans
豆 豉 (Dou-chi)

This is used to season steamed, sautéd or stewed fish and meat dishes. Ask for most recent processed ones; if stale it has a strong smell.

Fermented Horse Bean Paste
辣 酱 (La-jiang), 豆 板 酱 (Dou-ban-jiang)

Both contain chili pepper. The paste is made from horse beans or unrefined soybeans. Used for seasoning meat, vegetable and bean curd dishes.

Five-Spice Powder
五 香 粉 (Wu-xiang-fen)

Consists of ground star anise, cinnamon, cloves, Szechwan pepper and dried tangerine peels. Used in stewed meat dishes. Other than the above, pepper, cinnamon, curry powder, mustard, cloves, and nutmeg are used as needed.

Five-Spice Salt

五 香 盐 (Wu-xiang-yan)

Five-Spice Powder mixed with salt. Set at table.

Oyster Sauce and Shrimp Sauce

蚝 油 (Hao-you), 虾 油 (Xia-you)

Oysters or shrimps are preserved in salt, fermented, then skimmed. Often used to season elaborate dishes using beef, abalone, etc.

Sesame Oil

麻 油 (Ma-you)

This sesame oil is used in vinegar dishes. Sprinkle a little of it mixed with some spices over sautéd and steamed dishes. This is also used to sauté kidney to rid it of its strong taste.

Sesame Oil with Chili Pepper

辣 油 (La-you)

It is commonly used in fried dishes mixed with soy sauce and vinegar. Available in small bottles.

To make at home:

Mince 3 red chili peppers, seeds and all, and mix into 1 cup of hot sesame oil. Reheat a little while, let cool and strain to obtain a translucent red liquid. Be careful not to overheat or oil will turn black.

Sesame Sauce

芝 麻 酱 (Zhi-ma-jiang)

This is used in vinegared vegetable and meat dishes and as a sauce for pot dishes; it has a smell of sesame seeds. Be sure to ask for most recent processed ones.

Star Anise
八角茴香 (Ba-jiao-hui-xiang)

Looks like a flower and has seeds enclosed in its shell. Has a strong fragrance, used in stewed or steamed dishes of meat and fish.

Szechwan Pepper
花 椒 (Hua-jiao)

Dried Szechwan pepper seeds are used whole in stewed meat dishes and in pickled vegetables. Ground seeds are used to make Szechwan Pepper Salt or to season sautéd dishes.

Szechwan Pepper Salt
花 椒 盐 (Hua-jiao-yan)

Szechwan pepper seeds are crushed, ground and put through a fine sieve, then mixed with salt. They are used to season deep-fried fish or meat. If not kept covered, the pepper salt will absorb moisture.

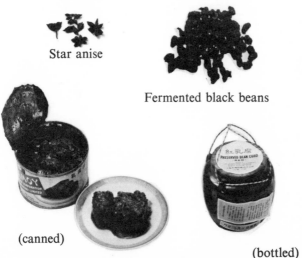

Star anise

Fermented black beans

(canned)

Fermented bean curd

(bottled)

Special Foods

Chinese Mushrooms

冬 菇 (Dong-gu), 花 菇 (Hua-gu), 香 菇 (Xiang-gu)

Highest quality mushrooms harvested in autumn are called dong-gu. Flower-like type is called huo-ga; it has a sweet fragrance and is also known as xiang-gu. This is a must in Chinese cooking.

How to prepare dried type:

Soak for about 1 hour in warm or cold water. Use liquid in soups.

Dried Abalone

干 鲍 (Gan-bao)

This is widely used in hors d'oeuvre, stewed, sautéd, steamed dishes and soups. Canned abalone is also available for easier preparation.

How to prepare:

After boiling for about 30 minutes, scrub well with a brush. Remove mouth section; simmer over low heat until soft. Liquid is excellent in soups.

Dried Bamboo Shoots

干 笋 (Gan-sun)

Used in noodles and sautéd dishes; salted and canned varieties are available.

How to prepare salted type:

Pour boiling water over and wash well, changing water frequently. Boil until soft.

Dried Sea Cucumber

海 参 (Hai-shen)

Often used in stewed dishes.

How to prepare:

Soak in hot water overnight; wash well. Slice smooth stomach portion lengthwise in half and remove entrails. Wash. Add water and cook until soft.

Dried Scallops

干 贝 (Gan-bei)

These are noted for their rich flavor.

How to prepare:

Soak in a large amount of hot water for about 2 hours. Use liquid as a broth. If you prefer it softer, pour liquid and scallops into a bowl, add a little dry sherry and steam for about 1 hour.

Dried Shrimps

虾 米 (Xia-mi)

Dried, shelled small shrimps make a good broth when used in soups and stewed dishes. Minced shrimps are used in stewed dishes.

How to prepare:

Rinse well and soak in hot or cold water.

Fungus

木 耳 (Mu-er), 银 耳 (Yin-er)

Both black and white mushroom varieties are available. The former is used in soups, sautéd dishes; white variety, Yin-er, is highly prized and used in soups and beverages.

How to prepare:

Soak in warm water, wash and remove stems.

Jellyfish

海 蜇 皮 (Hai-zhe-pi)

Used in vinegared dishes as an hors d'oeuvre.

How to prepare:

Soak the shredded type in water for half a day; pour boiling water over, then soak in water. Soak large pieces longer in water, then follow the above procedure.

Pickled Green

榨 菜 (Zha-cai)

From the Szechwan district; a kohlrabi vegetable that is preserved with chili pepper; eaten as pickled vegetable or used in sautéd dishes or soups. Use after washing off red coating.

Preserved Eggs

皮 蛋 (Pi-dan)

Also called 松 花 蛋 (Song-hua-dan), duck eggs are preserved in a special preparation. Remove coating, wash well, shell and cut into fourths.

Salted Eggs

咸 蛋 (Xian-dan)

Salted duck eggs. Remove and wash off coating. Boil and serve.

Shark's Fin

鱼 翅 (Yu-chi)

This is valued next to the above. Can be bought dried but preparation requires much time. Thus for home use, the shredded type is available.

How to prepare shredded Shark's fin:

Place in a bowl and pour boiling water over; let cool and then wash. Simmer in a large amount of water for about 1 hour. Rinse and use in soups, stewed and sautéd dishes. Canned fin is pre-cooked and may be used as it is.

Swallow's Nest

燕 窩 (Yan-wo)

The nest is found on cliffs by the sea and is prized highly by the Chinese. It is made from seaweed and resembles string-like gelatin. Soak in water to soften and carefully remove sediment and feathers with tweezers. Used in soups.

Vermicelli

粉 丝 (Fen-si)

Resembles Japanese vermicelli but is made from mung beans. It is firmer and does not get mushy. Used in pot dishes, soups, deep-fried and vinegared dishes. *How to prepare:*

Soak in warm water; cut into bite-sized lengths and use in soups or pot dishes. For use in vinegared dishes, boil before using.

How to Use Chopsticks

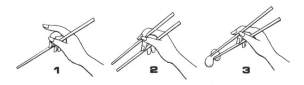

1. Place one of the chopsticks between thumb and tip of ring finger; lightly press.
2. Place the other chopstick as you would a pencil.
3. Do not move the first chopstick; move the second stick between index and middle fingers in an up and down motion to catch food.

How to Cut the Ingredients

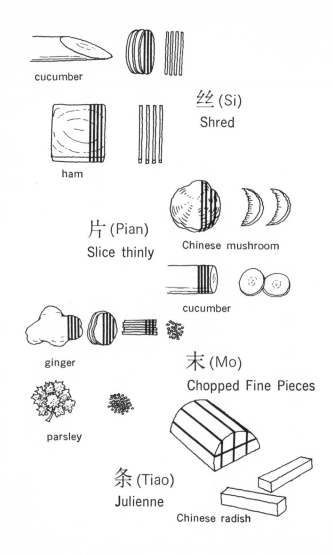

cucumber

丝 (Si)
Shred

ham

片 (Pian)
Slice thinly

Chinese mushroom

cucumber

ginger

末 (Mo)
Chopped Fine Pieces

parsley

条 (Tiao)
Julienne

Chinese radish

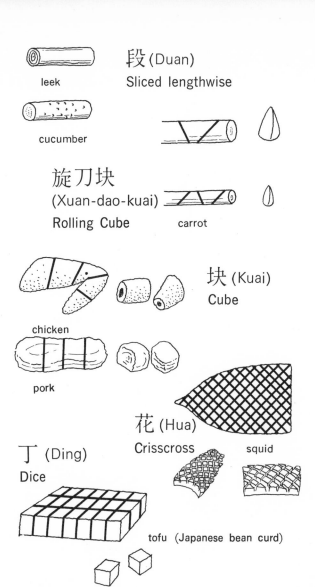

段 (Duan)
Sliced lengthwise

leek

cucumber

旋刀块
(Xuan-dao-kuai)
Rolling Cube

carrot

块 (Kuai)
Cube

chicken

pork

花 (Hua)
Crisscross

squid

丁 (Ding)
Dice

tofu (Japanese bean curd)

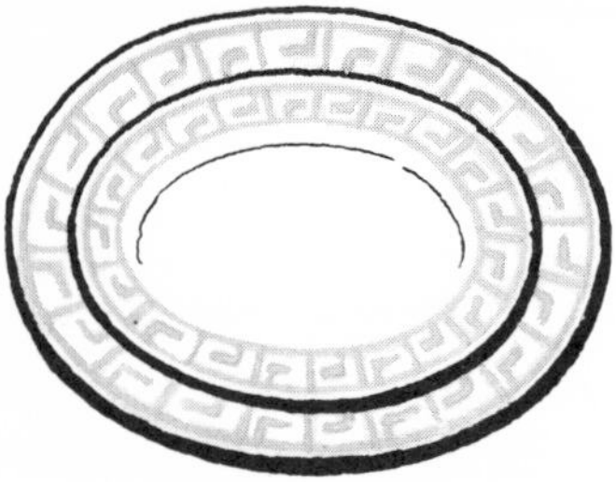

2 wide plates
(hors d'oeuvre, sautéd
food, deep-fried foods)

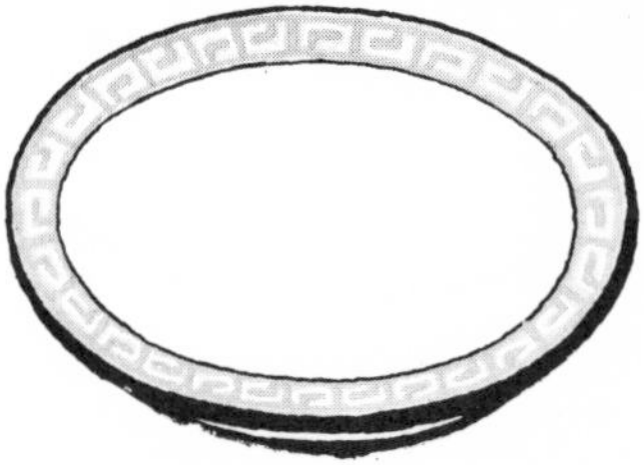

Deep plate
(stewed, steamed foods)

Rice bowl

Soup bowl

Porcelain spoon

Platter
(chicken, fish)

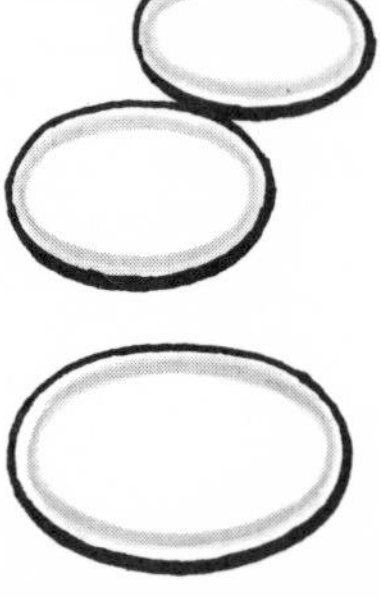

Individual serving dishes
(large, medium and small)

Chinese Dishes

Deep bowl
(soups, steamed foods)

Noodle bowl
(noodles with soup)

Hexagonal Plate

Tureen with lid

Cloud-shaped platter

Hors d'oeuvre plate

Utensils to Have on Hand

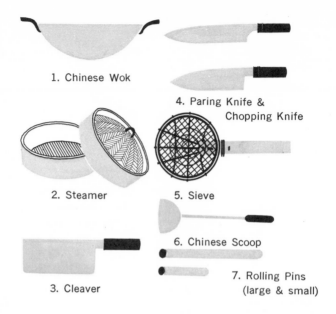

1. Chinese Wok

4. Paring Knife & Chopping Knife

2. Steamer

5. Sieve

6. Chinese Scoop

7. Rolling Pins (large & small)

3. Cleaver

♥ Usage
♠ After Use
♣ Purchasing Guide

1. Chinese Wok

♥ For deep-frying, pan-frying, steaming, and practically for all purposes. Bottom is curved so that it heats up well. When deep-frying, only a little oil is needed. Pan-frying requires less time because of the curved bottom. Pour in lots of hot water, bring to a boil and pour out, and towel dry. Heat and add oil.

♣ Choose size to suit home burners: size 12- or 14-inch wok is generally used.

♠ Scrub soiled portions; wash with hot water; heat until all moisture has evaporated.

94

2. Steamer

♥ May be used simply by arranging on top of the wok for all steamed dishes. The round cover is woven bamboo so the amount of boiling water is controlled directly and the heat circulates. Beads of moisture drip down the sides of the cover instead of directly onto the food.

The surface of the water is separated from the bottom of the steamer. Since the bottom rack of the steamer is also bamboo, the steamed foods will not get mushy. If the hot water in the wok evaporates, simply pour in more around the edge. When done, just remove steamer from the wok. Remove foods.

♣ Choose size according to the size of the wok. It should be just a little smaller than the wok. You may put layers of steamers on top of the other and thus save time in process, so one cover and two steamers are convenient to have on hand.

♠ Scrub greased steaming rack with detergent, rinse well and drain. Then set both cover and steamer in a breezy place to dry. Store in a plastic bag.

3. Cleaver

♥ Wide-bladed kitchen tool shaped like a hatchet. It is used for chopping through bones or for pounding meat thin.

♣ A good cleaver has a clear tone when the blade is flipped.

♠ Wash carefully and wipe dry.

4. Paring and Chopping Knives

♥ Paring knife may be used to peel and pare vegetables and for slicing meat and fish. Do not use to chop through bones or blade will get nicked. To fillet fish and chop unboned meat, a chopping knife is a must.

♣ It is enough to have both paring and chopping knives. Stainless steel will not rust as easily as iron; however, iron cuts better. About 8-inch size is handy to use.

♠ When used in cutting foods with a strong odor or natural tart taste, wash carefully and wipe dry.

5. Sieve
♥ Small or large, they are handy when deep-frying or boiling. Large ones are especially convenient for removing whole chicken or fish when deep-frying; small ones for small deep-fried or boiled foods.

♣ Select those with a long enough handle and sturdy frame.

♠ If left greasy, dust will adhere to the mesh and it will be hard to clean. Set in detergent suds and scrub; wash off any grease on handle. Rinse well and drain.

6. Chinese Scoop or Ladle
♥ For pan-frying.

♣ Round, long handle makes it easy to grasp. Select one with a rounded bowl.

♠ Scrub in detergent suds, wash both bowl portion and handle. Rinse, drain and towel dry.

7. Rolling Pins (Large and Small)
♥ For making noodles, cakes, fried and steamed meat dumpling wrappers.

♣ About 20-inch size is needed for noodles and steamed meat dumpling wrappers. About 7-inch size is used for cakes and fried meat dumpling wrappers.

♠ Wash with water, making sure that no trace of flour remains, and wrap in a dry towel.

Index

Abalone, dried   86
Almond Flavored Gelatin   78–79

Bamboo Shoots, dried   86
Bananas, Frosty   80

Cantonese, regional food of the south   6
Chicken:
    Oriental Crisp Chicken   50–53
    Steamed Chicken   16, 19
    with Green Peas   40, 41
Chinese beverages   14
Chinese mushrooms   86
Chinese noodles, making   81–82
Chinese Pot   58–61
Chopsticks, using   89
Chop Suey   26–29
Chow Mein   66–67
Cleaver, buying and caring for   95
Colorful Vinegared Dish   30–33
Crisp Fish with Sweet Sour Sauce   34–37
Crisp Meatballs   54–57
Crisp Shrimp Cakes   76–77
Cutting ingredients for recipes   90–91

Deep-frying   9, 36
Dried abalone   86
Dried bamboo shoots   86
Dumplings, Steamed Meat   72–75

Eggs:
    Egg Foo Young   62–65
    Fried Rice with Egg   68–71
    preserved eggs   88
    salted eggs   88
    Steamed Eggs   24–25
    Stewed Boiled Eggs   18, 19

Fermented bean curd   83
Fermented black beans   83
Fermented horse bean paste   83
Fish with Sweet Sour Sauce   34–37

Five-spice powder   83
Five-spice salt   84
Fried Rice with Egg   68–71
Frosty Bananas   80
Fungus   87

Gelatin, Almond Flavored   78–79
Green Peas, Shrimps with   38–41
Grilled Flavored Pork   42–45
Grilling   10

Hangchow, regional food of the east central   6
Hors d'oeuvre, preparing and serving   16

Jellyfish   88

Lard, rendering   70

Meatballs:
    Crisp Meatballs   54–57
    Meatball Soup   56
    Sweet Sour Meatballs   56
Meat Dumplings, Steamed   72–75
Mushrooms, Chinese   86

Noodles:
    dried noodles, preparing   82
    fresh noodles, making   81–82
    steamed noodles, preparing   82

Oil for deep-frying   36
One-Pot Dish (with meatballs)   56
Oriental Crisp Chicken   50–53
Oyster Sauce   84
Oyster Soup   20–23

Pan-frying   9
Paring and chopping knives, caring for   95–96
Peas, Chicken with Green   40, 41
Peking, regional food of the north   5
Pepper, Szechwan   85
Pepper salt, Szechwan   85
Pickled Green   88
Pork, Grilled Flavored   42–45

Prawns, Fried   18, 19
Preserved eggs   88

Regional foods of China   5–6
Rice, Fried with Egg   68–71
Rolling pins, buying and caring for   96

Salted eggs   88
Sautéing   9
Scoop, buying and caring for   96
Scallops, dried   87
Sea Cucumber, dried   87
Seasoned meat   54
Serving platters and bowls   92–93
Sesame oil   84
Sesame oil with chili pepper   84
Sesame sauce   84
Shanghai, regional food of the east central   6
Shantung, regional food of the north   5
Shao Mai wrappers, making   74–75
Shark's fin   88
Shrimp:
    Crisp Shrimp Cakes   76–77
    with Green Peas   38–41
    with Soy Beans   40–41
Shrimp sauce   84
Shrimps, dried   87
Soups, types of   11
Soy Beans, Shrimps with   40, 41
Star Anise   85
Steamed Cakes   80
Steamed Chicken   18, 19
Steamed Eggs   24–25
Steamer, buying and caring for   95
Steaming   10
Stewed Boiled Eggs   18, 19
Stewed dishes   10
Szechwan, regional food of the west   5
Szechwan pepper   85

Szechwan pepper salt   85

Swallow's nest   89

Sweet Sour Pork   46–49

Sweet Sour Sauce, Crisp Fish with   34–37

Tea   15

Utensils, buying and caring for   94–96

Vermicelli   89

Vinegared Dish, Colorful   30–33

Wok, buying and caring for   94